VANGUARD SERIES

EDITOR: MARTIN WINDROW

SOVIET HEAVY TANKS

Text by

STEVEN J. ZALOGA and JAMES GRANDSEN

Colour plates by

STEVEN J. ZALOGA

OSPREY PUBLISHING LONDON

Published in 1981 by
Osprey Publishing Ltd
Member company of the George Philip Group
12–14 Long Acre, London WC2E 9LP
© Copyright 1981 Osprey Publishing Ltd
Reprinted 1985

ISBN 0 85045 422 0

Filmset in Great Britain
Printed in Hong Kong

In memory of my brother Jack
S.Z.

Genesis of the Leviathans

The last of the multi-turreted behemoths built for the Red Army, the T-35 Model 1938 differed from earlier models in having sloped turret armour for slightly better ballistic protection. Here tanks of the 34th Tank Div. parade in Red Square on 7 November 1940. (Sovfoto)

After the German-Soviet alliance of 1939, Soviet delegations visited German armament factories and examined the latest in German weapons. In spring 1941 a team headed by I. F. Tevosian visited German tank factories producing the most modern designs, including the PzKpfw IV. The Germans hoped that this confident display of military strength would intimidate the Russians, much as it had the earlier US delegation led by Charles Lindbergh. The Germans were taken aback when the Soviets bitterly asked why they had not been allowed to see any heavy tanks or anything more modern than the PzKpfw IV. The Werhmacht attributed this outburst to the usual Russian suspiciousness. Col. Kinzel, head of the Intelligence section responsible for monitoring Soviet weapons development, assured his colleagues that while there were Finnish reports of a curious multi-turreted tank being knocked out during the 1940 war, it was nothing more than a derivative of the antiquated T-35, and certainly nothing to be afraid of. A month later Operation 'Barbarossa' confirmed the inadequacies of German Intelligence: reports, which verged on panic, spoke of the massive 50-ton tanks impervious to the fire of the PzKpfw IV, tanks which mockingly defied the Wehrmacht's 37mm anti-tank gun by grinding it beneath its tracks. The Wehrmacht had just encountered the KV heavy tank, probably the most feared weapon in the Russian arsenal of 1941.

★   ★   ★

During the early years of the Second World War, the Red Army was the only force to possess any number of heavy tanks. (The French had fielded six 1920-vintage Char lourd 2C in 1940, but these dinosaurs did not see action as they had been destroyed on rail cars during transit to the front.) The first Soviet heavy tanks were developed in the early 1930s as part of the First Five Year Plan. Their construction had as much to do with propaganda as with any real military value. The Red Army liked to portray itself as the

3

The combat career of the T-35 was brief and unremarkable. Most of the multi-turreted battleships fell victim to their own mechanical unreliability, and were abandoned during the calamitous frontier battles of June 1941 in the Ukraine, like this T-35 Mod.1935. The engine cover has been removed in a vain attempt to repair it. The significance of the hastily-painted white triangles on hull and turrets is unknown. (James Crow)

avant garde in military technology, and the sight of a battalion of gargantuan 50-ton tanks clanking through Red Square every May Day served this purpose admirably.

In 1930 two design teams belonging to N. Barykov's Experimental Design Unit (OKMO) at the Bolshevik Factory in Leningrad began work on two heavy tank designs. The team headed by an engineer named Grote undertook construction of a superheavy, five-turreted monstrosity named the TG-5 (later the T-42). This tank was to weigh about 100 tons, mounting a 107mm gun in its main turret, two more turrets with 37mm guns, and a pair of smaller machine gun turrets. Grote later made the dubious claim that the prototype was completed, but the design was clearly outside the technical capability of Russia's fledgling heavy industry. A second team headed by N. Tsiets initiated work on a more practical design obviously based on the British Independent. This vehicle, named T-35, also had five turrets, but was of more modest size than the

reputed T-42, and was more thinly armoured and lightly armed. In July 1932 the prototype began construction, and it underwent trials the following April; it was rushed to Moscow in time for the 1933 May Day parade. As an outcome of this display a special meeting of the Economics and Defence Council was held, and it was decided to adopt the T-35 for use in the Red Army. Production was eventually to take place at the Kharkov Locomotive Factory im. Komintern. A pre-production batch of about ten vehicles was manufactured shortly afterwards. The main turret held a 76.2mm PS-3 howitzer, derived from the stubby Model 27 regimental gun, and also mounted a forward-firing machine gun and a rear machine gun for AA defence. Surrounding the main turret were four smaller sub-turrets which had only 180° traverse. Two, one fore and one aft, were armed with 37mm B-3 tank guns derived from the German 37mm Rheinmetall weapon. The others held Degtaryev DT machine guns; and a fifth MG was located in the hull front. A second batch of ten tanks was completed in Kharkov with an improved turret; this also had a special roof mount for an anti-aircraft MG.

The best known version of the series, the T-35 Model 1935, entered production in 1935, and about 35 were built by 1938. This longer version had eight road wheels per side. The hull front had been redesigned, the hull MG discarded, and the armament improved. The main armament was the L-10 76.2mm gun derived from the improved Model 27/32 regimental gun. The old 37mm turrets were replaced by cylindrical turrets nearly identical to those on the T-26 and BT light tanks, armed with a 45mm Model 1934 tank gun. There were two-man crews in the new turrets, raising the complement to 11 crewmen and the weight to 45 tons. These vehicles, as befitted a land battleship, were amply provided with ammunition, carrying 96–100 rounds of 76.2mm, 225 rounds of 45mm and 9,230 rounds of machine gun ammunition. Finally, in 1938 a small run of about six T-35 Model 1938s were built. These had redesigned turret armour angled to give better ballistic protection, and incorporated a number of other small design changes. This brought total T-35 production to 61 vehicles when production was halted in 1939.

By this point it was obvious that the T-35's 20–30mm armour was vulnerable to the new generation of anti-tank guns used during the Spanish Civil War. Nor had the T-35 proved to be particularly well thought-out, from either the technical or operational standpoints. Its M-17 gasoline engine was overworked and capricious, prone to breakdown and fires. It suffered the transmission problems that were the trademark of Soviet tanks of the period; this was doubly serious as the ratio between track width and length of ground contact was so high that it was difficult to steer the vehicle and very easy to shed a track. Repairing the track was a nightmare, both because of its length and weight, and because of the height of the upper trackrun from the ground.

The land-battleship notion held great appeal for 'armchair generals', but was tactically foolish and an operational headache. In order to work effectively the vehicle commander would have had to have fire controls akin to those on a small destroyer, such as turret direction indicators, and good inter-turret communication equipment. No such equipment was present; moreover, the T-35 main turret was laid out in traditional Russian fashion. Not only did the commander have to control his driver and his turret gunners, he was also responsible for loading the 76.2mm main gun and the frontal DT machine gun! It was not surprising if the commander sank into apoplexy when it is realised that since the tank lacked any form of gun stabilisation it had to be ordered to a halt every time any one of the three main guns wanted to fire.

Initially the T-35s were allotted to two independent battalions under the command of Supreme Command Reserve, but during the 1938 re-organisation of the armoured force they were amalgamated into the 5th Heavy Tank Brigade. Three similar brigades were also formed at the time, but lacking any more heavy tanks these units were equipped with the T-28 medium tank. The T-28 resembled the T-35 in that it was equipped with the same main and MG turrets, but it lacked the two 45mm gun turrets. The nominal strength of the 5th Heavy Tank Brigade was 94 T-35s, 44 BT Betushka fast tanks and ten flamethrower tanks. Since there were less than 60 running T-35s available the unit was fleshed out with T-28 medium tanks. Of the three battalions, the separate heavy tank training battalion was used every year at the May Day and November 7th parades in Moscow. Interestingly enough this unit was commanded by Sergei M. Shtemenko, who served as Deputy Chief of General Headquarters during the Second World War and later became Chief of Staff of the Soviet Armed Forces. During another re-organisation of the armoured forces in 1940 the surviving runners of the T-35 battalions served with the 34th Tank Division of the 8th Mechanised Corps. Considered the best tank division in the Red Army, this was wiped out in heavy fighting in the Ukraine in 1941 during the huge armour battle around Brody and Dubno. The fate of the T-35s during these battles is unrecorded by the Russians, although there is extensive German photographic coverage of these curious gargantuans. From these photos it would appear that few were knocked out during fighting, and most were probably abandoned due to breakdowns and lack of fuel. Some T-35s survived around Moscow and took part in the defence of the capital in winter 1941. One abandoned by the Red Army near Lvov was apparently recruited into the Ukrainian nationalist OUN partisan force in

This T-35 Mod.1938 apparently served the Ukrainian nationalist cause for a short time in late summer 1941 before being abandoned near Lvov in October. The slogan is 'Glory to Stepan Bandera', referring to the leader of the Ukrainian OUN movement, and below it is the 'trident of Volodymyr' emblem; round the drive sprocket is painted 'Glory to the Ukraine'. (James Crow)

autumn 1941 before finally being abandoned outside the city.

In spite of the less than inspiring service career of the T-35, the Red Army was firmly wedded to the dramatic appeal of the multi-turreted land battleship. In 1937 the Directorate of the Armoured and Mechanised Forces (ABTU) laid plans for an 'Anti-tank Gun Destroyer' able to withstand the fire of 37–45mm anti-tank guns at point-blank range, or the fire of 75mm field guns at 1,200 metres. That such an anachronistic conception was still entertained demonstrates how misunderstood were the experiences of the Soviet tank force in Spain. The project was to be competitively developed by a team led by the former head of OKMO, N. Barykov, and another led by Zhozef Kotin. Barykov headed the team at the Bolshevik Factory (subsequently renamed S. M. Kirov Factory No. 185); Kotin headed that team at the Kirovski Works, formerly the Putilov Works, which had produced armoured vehicles under the Tsar. (Kotin was a young protégé of Marshal Mikhail Tukhachevsky, First Deputy Commissar for Defence and the driving force

behind the Red Army's mechanisation programme; the Marshal's execution during the purges was but the most grievous example of the self-inflicted butchery that crippled the Red Army in the years before the war.)

The Barykov team's design was called T-100, or *Sotka*—slang for '100'. The Kotin team followed the current Leningrad fad for naming everything after the deceased party boss S. M. Kirov—the 'SMK'. The specifications called for five turrets, though the engineers quickly convinced the Defence Council to reduce this to three by eliminating the 'decorative' MG turrets. On 4 May 1938 the designs were shown to a special meeting of the Defence Council in Moscow. Kotin brashly questioned the utility of three turrets, which provoked Stalin to go up to one of the wooden models, break off one of the turrets and quip: 'Why make a tank into a department store!' This helped ameliorate one of the problems, but the Defence Council soon became enmeshed in another. In the wake of the purges a crony of Stalin's, G. Kulik, became head of the artillery branch. Kulik was a vociferous ignoramus, and during a technical discussion of problems in producing armour plate thicker than 60mm for tanks he backed the quack theories of a former tanker from Spain who claimed that laminate armour was the answer. Several engineers had to literally risk their necks to reverse Stalin's decision to use this armour on the T-100 and SMK. The May meeting also resulted in the Defence Council's acquiesence to the design teams' request to use novel torsion bar suspension on the SMK instead of older spring suspensions.

Kotin and his assistant Yermolayev were still unhappy even with two turrets, and on their own initiative designed a single-turreted version of the SMK. Kotin won Stalin's approval for the design at an August 1938 meeting of the Central Committee at which the projected tank was named 'KV' after Stalin's crony Marshal Klimenti Voroshilov, the People's Defence Commissar. Two T-100 prototypes were built, each weighing about 58 tons and crewed by seven men. There were two turrets, the uppermost armed with a short L-11 76.2mm gun and the lower with a 45mm Model 1938. The SMK was of similar configuration with the same armament. The two KV prototypes resembled stubbier, single-turret versions of the SMK. In December 1939, following a series of proving grounds trials which greatly favoured the KV, all the prototypes were sent to the Finnish front for operational trials. Formed as a special company of the 20th Armd. Bde. and commanded by Major P. Voroshilov, son of the Defence Commissar, they were used in a number of different skirmishes, mainly against Finnish fortifications around Summa. The SMK was knocked out by a large mine and abandoned. The earlier tests were confirmed, and on 19 December 1939 the Defence Committee ordered acceptance of the KV, and initial production of 50 tanks at the Kirovski Works during 1940.

The troop trials in Finland revealed the difficulties of dealing with reinforced bunkers with ordinary tank guns. The commander of the 7th Army, Gen. K. Meretskov, requested crash production of a howitzer tank mounting a 152–203mm weapon. Three programmes were hastily undertaken, though only one was completed in time to serve in Finland.

A 130mm B-13 high-velocity naval gun was mounted into a fixed casemate mount on one of the T-100 prototypes, called the T-100U (U: *Ulukhshonniy* = Improved). This was not finished in time but later served during the defence of Moscow in the winter of 1941 as the SU-100Y. There was a similar attempt to mount either a

152mm Br-2 or 203mm B-4 howitzer into a modified KV hull called by its factory designation Obiekt 212, or SU-212, but this was never finished due to the outbreak of war with Germany. The third project mounted a modified 152mm howitzer into an enlarged KV turret; rushed to Finland, it fought in February around Summa. Gen. Meretskov noted its excellent performance in destroying bunkers, and urged the Defence Council to push it into production. This version was originally called '*KV s bolshi bashni*' and the version with the 76mm gun '*KV s malenki bashni*' (Large Turret KV and Small Turret KV). However, Soviet tankers called the howitzer-armed version 'Dreadnought'. Later, when the howitzer version was accepted by the Red Army, the heavy tank version was called KV-1 and the howitzer version KV-2.

The two T-100 *Sotka* prototypes saw combat in Finland in December 1939, but their lacklustre performance led to the adoption of the KV instead. (Sovfoto)

Although the initial production schedule for the KV was for 50 vehicles in 1940, its success led to this being increased to 243 tanks, of which 141 were KV-1 and 102 were KV-2. The early production KVs were plagued by engine and transmission problems. The engine did not provide its rated horsepower and the vehicle was very difficult to steer. The KV-1 was scheduled to be fitted with the F-32 76.2mm gun being designed by the Grabin team at Artillery Zavod Nr. 92 in Gorki, but due to delays the short L-11 gun was used on the initial production run. Curiously enough the Grabin bureau was also developing an improved gun for the new T-34 medium tank, called the F-34. The F-34 was still under test as the F-32 was going into production, but eventually followed in the spring of 1941. This led to the curious situation of a medium tank having a somewhat better gun than its counterpart heavy tank. As a result, in 1941 it was decided to up-arm the KV-1 with a derivative of this gun, called the ZiS-5, though F-34 guns were often used since there was so little difference between them.

With production firmly established, the Kotin design team in Leningrad began working on future developments of the KV series. Paper studies were undertaken of the KV-4 and KV-5, 100-ton and 150-ton assault tanks, but these never advanced beyond feasibility studies. The KV-3 was a more serious effort aimed at examining the most practical path for maturing the KV design. The KV-3 project actually encompassed two very different designs, called by their factory designations Obiekt 220 and Obiekt 222. The Obiekt 222 design was essentially a modestly updated KV-1 with thicker armour and a re-

designed turret giving the tank commander a vision cupola. Obiekt 220, a more elaborate effort, had a new engine in a lengthened hull, and a new gun in a cut-down KV-2 turret. This was supposed to be the new 85mm F-39 under design at the Grabin bureau. Before these plans were realised the upper echelons of the Red Army were wracked by another pointless imbroglio. The idiot artillery chief, Kulik, had unveiled his latest hare-brained premonition to the members of the Defence Council. According to his 'sources' the Wehrmacht was up-armouring its tanks with 100mm armour plate or more. This being the case, all Soviet anti-tank guns including the superb new ZiS-2 57mm gun and the new 76.2mm tank guns were now worthless. Kulik suggested that all production of these weapons be stopped in favour of a new 107mm gun. Stalin concurred in spite of the protests of several council members. Needless to say, this information was complete rubbish, and the April 1941 factory orders had appalling effects on the production of vitally needed tank and anti-tank guns. The immediate

Axis cameramen recording close-ups of the KV-2 at Rasyeinyia after its eventual capture.

effect on the KV-3 programme was to delay work on the armament. The Grabin bureau had quickly to develop a 107mm gun to suit Kulik's mandate; the tank version, the ZiS-6, was completed in May 1941 but was never mounted in the KV-3 due to the outbreak of the war. The KV-3 prototype was later armed with an 85mm or 100mm naval gun and took part in the defence of Leningrad.

At the time of the outbreak of war on 22 June 1941 there were 508 KVs in service with Red Army tank divisions. The divisions had been re-organised in June 1940 in the wake of the stunning German victory over France. Stalin had ordered the disbandment of the previous mechanised corps in November 1939, following the advice from his cronies that such units were ineffective and could be better employed scattered through the infantry and cavalry divisions in small units. The new 1940 tank divisions were in turn organised into mechanised corps consisting of two tank divisions and one motorised division, totalling some 1,031 tanks. The tank divisions had a nominal strength of 63 KV heavy tanks, 210 T-34 mediums and 102 old T-26 or BT 'sparrow shooters'. The 1940 plans called for the formation of 29 mechanised corps with 61 tank divisions—wildly optimistic, considering the state of the Soviet armoured park.

Soviet heavy industry during the two Five Year Plans had undertaken the staggering task of mechanising the enormous Red Army and building the largest tank force in the world. Soviet tank production greatly exceeded the production of all other countries combined. However, the Soviet fascination with impressive production figures did not extend to the more mundane subject of tank maintenance or manufacture of spare parts. As a result, by 1941 the huge Soviet tank park of 22,000–24,000 vehicles was largely immobile: 44 per cent of the tanks required rebuilding, and 29 per cent required replacement of a major component such as an engine or transmission. There were no parts available for such repairs. The 'sparrow-shooters' that were still running through cannibalisation were themselves ripe for mechanical breakdown. The new tank divisions enthusiastically welcomed the T-34s and KVs, but many units received only

This KV-2 Mod.1939 of the 5th Tank Div. rests in a shallow emplacement near Alitus, Lithuania, during the June 1941 battles. This variant of the Dreadnought had a more complex turret than the standard production model, and only a handful were built. (National Archives)

token amounts, which arrived so late that there was no time to train on them. There was only a tenth of the 76.2mm tank ammunition needed, and no one had informed some of the units receiving the KV-2 that they were expected to use old 03–90 152mm concrete-bursting ammunition in lieu of armour-piercing rounds. In spite of these daunting handicaps most Soviet tank crews were cocky and confident, if for no other reason than their highly-praised performances in the artificial and meaningless summer wargames, or their performance against the poorly equipped Japanese in the Far East in 1938 and 1939.

Débâcle on the Frontiers

The nine Soviet mechanised corps that were in some state of readiness were encamped over 70km from the frontier when the first German attacks were launched on 22 June 1941. The first serious engagements between KVs and Panzers took place in Lithuania the following day. Col.Gen. F. I. Kuznetsov's North-West Front had two partially equipped Mechanised Corps, the 3rd commanded by Maj.Gen. Kurkin and the 12th commanded by Maj.Gen. Shestopalov. The 3rd Mechanised Corps was immediately divided up: the 2nd Tank Div. was sent along with the 12th Mechanised Corps up towards the Dubissa River to stop the German advance along the main

This lone KV-2 Mod. 1940 of the 2nd Tank Div. held off repeated attacks by 6th Panzer Div. near the Rasyeinyia crossroads in Lithuania. The damage caused by the engineer demolition charges on the right track is evident here. (James Crow)

Tilsit-Shauliya highway, the 84th Motorised Div. was kept as 11th Army reserve, and the 5th Tank Div. rushed south to the border town of Alitus. After a forced march of 80km, the 28th Tank Div. of the 12th Mechanised Corps began its attacks against the 1st Panzer Div. 50km south of Shauliya to the west of the main highway. Heavier fighting engulfed the 2nd Tank Div., commanded by Gen. E. N. Solyalyankin, which ran head-on into lead elements of the 4th Panzer Group along the main highway. An attack was immediately launched by about 80 BT light tanks supported by a small number of T-34s and 20 KVs. The Germans began blasting away at the KVs with their 37mm PAK 36 anti-tank guns, only to watch in dismay as the shells harmlessly bounced off. More frightening was the fact that 75mm fire from the 'Stubs' (PzKpfw IVs with short 75mm guns) also proved ineffective. The 2nd Tank Div. claimed 40 Panzers destroyed, and an equal number of guns, many of which were 37mms that had simply been run over and crushed.

The 2nd Tank Div. withdrew from the battlefield around Skaudvilye by midday, to meet up with the 12th Mechanised Corps north of Rasyeinyia. By this time the division was nearly out of fuel and ammunition, and many of the older tanks were in bad mechanical condition due to the forced march. The division reached the fields above the Dubissa River, but were threatened by the advance of the 6th Panzer Div., which had already seized Rasyeinyia and had at least two bridgeheads over the Dubissa. The bridgeheads were attacked, and Gen. Solyalyankin sent a single KV-2 and some infantry past the German positions on the river to sever their road connections with the rest of 6th Panzer in Rasyeinyia. There was one battalion of Pz35(t)s at the northern bridgehead near Lydaverai, and another battalion further down the river. On the afternoon of 23 June the Lydaverai battalion realised it had been cut off, and sent some of the anti-tank guns from Pz.Jg.Abt. 41 and 105mm howitzers from Art. Regt. 76 to cover their southern flank in case the Russians tried to attack them from the rear. The next morning a relief column from Rasyeinyia tried to link up with the isolated battalion, but its 12 trucks were quickly blown apart by the KV-2, which had positioned itself to cover the fork in the road leading to both bridgeheads. Further attempts were equally fruitless, and the situation at the river was getting very precarious. The attacks on the isolated battalions were intense, and the 37mm gun of the PzKpfw 35(t) was worthless against the KVs. Only the 105mm howitzers of the artillery had any effect on the leviathans. The situation became so critical that 6th Panzer was obliged to request 1st Panzer to the west to begin attacks against the Russian flank.

In the afternoon a battery of brand new PAK 38 50mm anti-tank guns was carefully moved up towards the KV from the bridgehead. The lead gun was only 600 yards away when it began firing and was soon joined by the others. The KV-2 was not in the least disturbed by a direct hit, nor by the six other rounds that struck in quick succession. It destroyed the first gun with a direct hit, followed by several more rounds that damaged the other guns. In the meantime an 88mm Flak gun from Flak. Abt. 298 was carefully pulled out of its emplacement near Rasyeinyia and camouflaged with branches. The half-track towing it moved carefully behind the wrecked trucks for concealment and the crew hastily lowered the gun off its limbers. The activity had been spotted by the KV, and when the '88' was only 900 metres away the Russian gunner destroyed it and the tractor with two direct hits. Relief parties were kept away by machine gun fire. That night a squad from Pz.Pioniere Bn.57 crept up to the KV, placed a double charge of explosive against the hull, and detonated it—only

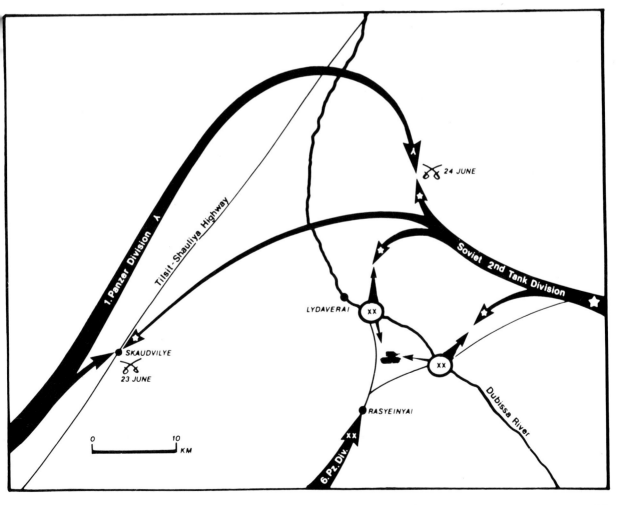

11

A KV-1 Mod.1940 passes into Palace Square, Leningrad in autumn 1941. The slogan reads 'We Defend the Conquests of October'—see Plate A2.

'The KV-1 and KV-2, which we first met here, were quite something. Our companies commenced firing at 800 metres but it was ineffective. We moved closer and closer . . . soon we faced each other at 50–100 metres. A fantastic exchange of fire took place without any German success . . . our armour-piercing rounds simply bounced off them. They drove right through us towards the infantry and rear services. We turned around and followed behind, where we succeeded in knocking some of them out with special-purpose rounds (Pzgr 40) at very close range: 30–60 metres!' The artillery of the 6th Panzer Div. had positioned itself on the heights overlooking the battlefield and made up for the poor showing of the 35(t) tanks against the KVs. The PzKpfw 35(t)s took a heavy toll of the lighter BTs and T-26s. Caught between the two Panzer divisions, the remnants of the Russian force were pushed into the swamps where they were easy targets. By nightfall, nearly 180 burning Soviet tanks littered the battlefield.

Freed of the threat from the north, a platoon of PzKpfw 35(t)s was dispatched the next day from the bridgehead and worked its way to a small wood near the lone KV-2 at the crossroads. They kept up a steady stream of fire to distract the Russian crew while another 88mm gun was carefully brought up from Rasyeinyia. When in position it opened fire, scoring six direct hits. The tank crews dismounted to inspect the KV, which had not even burned. On reaching the tank they were appalled to notice that only two of the six 88mm rounds had penetrated the armour. There were seven small gouges from the 50mm strikes, but there was no damage evident from their 37mm guns. As a couple of the tankers climbed on board, the gun began moving towards them. An engineer who had accompanied them had the presence of mind to drop a couple of grenades through the holes in the turret rear, finally putting an end to this troublesome roadblock. This single KV had played a prominent rôle in delaying the advance of Panzergruppe 4 on Leningrad by forcing the diversion of the 1st Panzer Div. from its rapid drive to help out 6th Panzer, and prevented the destruction of the immobile 2nd Tank Division, if only for a day.

This was hardly the last KV that Panzergruppe 4 would encounter. Due to the proximity

to duck as the KV began spraying the area with machine gun fire. A straggler from the team approached the vehicle and found that the charge had only broken the track and ripped up the fender without any effect on the armour. He placed a second small charge on the barrel, but this had negligible results.

While these futile attempts to clear the road to the Dubissa River were going on, the largest tank battle during the drive on Leningrad was taking place in the thick forests and swampy fields to the north. The 1st Panzer Div. had come to the rescue of 6th Panzer by striking the western flank of the 12th Mechanised Corps and 2nd Tank Division. During the attack Pz. Gren. Rgt. 113 of 1st Panzer was nearly overrun by KV-2s and attempts by Pz. Jg. Bn. 37 to stop them proved fruitless when the 'Dreadnoughts' simply ran their 37mm guns over. 1st Panzer was equipped largely with PzKpfw IIIs and IVs, and had a greater measure of success against the KVs than the ineffective PzKpfw 35(t)s of 6th Panzer. They were unable to penetrate the frontal armour of the KV, but under unusual circumstances could sometimes disable them. A tanker from Pz. Regt. 1 wrote of the 24 June encounter on the Dubissa:

of the Baltic states to the Leningrad factory where the KVs were manufactured, they turned up in much larger numbers during the autumn 1941 campaign in this region than in Byelorussia or the Ukraine. The KV also played a prominent rôle in the enormous tank mêlée at Brody-Dubno (see Vanguard No. 14, *The T-34 Tank*). But as at Rasyeinyia, they could not decisively affect the outcome of these battles in view of the serious shortcomings of the Red Army at the time; they could only force the Panzer regiments, and especially the ill-protected infantry, to pay a heavy price for their advance. The KV and its stablemate, the T-34, were not yet available in sufficient numbers, nor were they adeptly handled. Their crews were not yet trained, and the long forced marches to the frontier exacerbated the mechanical problems from which the early production batches suffered. Many were abandoned for lack of fuel or spares, and others were lost to air attack.

Most of the combat casualties were caused by German howitzers or 88mm guns. By July only handfuls of KVs were left of the original 500 in service in June. These were sent into action in small batches in the hope of securing local successes. The 3rd Tank Div. made a final disorganised counter-attack at Ostrov on 7 July, losing its last KV-2s. On 15 July, STAVKA (Soviet High Command) was obliged to recognise the obvious and disband the mechanised corps. Of the 22,000 tanks that had existed at the outset of Barbarossa, it is unlikely that there were many more than 1,500 still running.

The motorised divisions were turned into

The bulk of the KV-2 is evident in this photo of a captured Mod.1940 brought to the Krupp works at Essen in 1941, and used in April 1945 to defend the plant against advancing US tanks—with little success. The Germans made little use of captured KV-2s, although a special unit, zbV 66, was formed for the planned invasion of Malta, Operation 'Herkules', with up-armoured PzKpfw IVs, captured T-34s and some KV-2s with German commanders' cupolas added. (US Army)

KV-1 Mod.1941 of the 116th Tank Bde. photographed in 1942, its turret emblazoned 'For the Homeland!'; this brigade was one of the most photographed Soviet units in 1942, and its vehicles were gaudily decorated with patriotic slogans and the names of Russian heroes. (Sovfoto)

ordinary infantry divisions, and the tank divisions that had survived were doled out to support the efforts of local front commanders. Army commanders, appreciating the near invulnerability of the KV, pleaded for more. Maj.Gen. K. Rokossovski recalled in his memoirs: 'The KV tanks literally stunned the enemy. They withstood the fire of every type of gun that the German tanks were armed with. But what a sight they were on returning from combat. Their armour was pock-marked all over and sometimes even their barrels were pierced.' Gen. I. Kh. Bagramyan recalled an incident during the fighting inside the town of Berdichev by the 10th Tank Div. when a single KV-1 commanded by Lt. I. N. Zhalin knocked out eight German tanks, even though it had suffered over three dozen direct hits at very close range. In late July Lt.Gen. A. Yeremenko sent a report back to Col.Gen. D. G. Pavlov, commander of the Western Front: 'Handled by brave men, the KV tanks can do wonders. In the sector of the 107th Motorised Infantry Division we sent a KV to silence an enemy anti-tank battery. It squashed the artillery, rolled up and down the enemy's gun emplacements, was hit more than 200 times, but the armour was unpierced even though it had been the target of guns of all types. Often our tanks went out of action due to the hesitant and unsure conduct of their crews rather than direct hits. For this reason we subsequently manned the KV tanks with hand-picked crews.'

Yeremenko touched upon a factor that is not obvious when trying to evaluate a tank from data tables and dry statistics about armour thickness and gun performance. A tank can be vulnerable even if its armour is impervious, due to the frailties of its crew. An example of this occurred on 3 July when elements of the 12th Tank Regt. of the 1st Moscow Motor Rifle Div. clashed with the 18th Panzer Div. at Lipki near the Borisov bridgehead. A sally by T-62s and BTs led by a KV-2 and a T-34 attacked a mixed column of PzKpfw IIIs and IVs. The light tanks were quickly knocked out for the loss of one PzKpfw III. The T-34 was flanked, and a carefully placed shot blew away a track link, disabling it. The crew leapt from the relative security of their armour, and were mown down by machine gun fire. The KV-2 was repeatedly struck but not damaged by the German tank fire, but under the frightening pounding of the PzKpfw IV's HE rounds the crew panicked and baled out, only to suffer the same fate.

To withstand repeated concussive blows from enemy shells required either a special presence of mind, or an apathetic numbness induced by nervous exhaustion. An anti-tank round striking the turret would create such friction that even if it did not penetrate it would burn off the paint on the inside near the point of impact, with a stench that provided the crew with an unwelcome reminder of how close they had come to a brutal death. High-explosive rounds that did not penetrate made the turret resonate, causing nose and ear bleeding. The noise and shock of attack heightened natural claustrophobic fears at being confined within the dank interior of a machine laden with high explosive and diesel fuel and foul with cordite and engine fumes. Peering through the narrow field of view of a Russian PT-4-7 periscope while the tank lurched and bounced over rough terrain induced motion sickness and disorientation. It took little imagination for a crew to picture the results of an anti-tank round as it careered into a turret, spraying a stream of supersonic metal shards which ricocheted around the walls, making no distinction between steel and flesh. Ideally confined to do the worst possible damage, they would eventually strike ammunition, causing the tank to explode as its

Platoon of KV-1s Mod.1941 of 1st Bn., 116th Tank Bde., lined up for inspection in March 1942. From the initial production batch, these tanks have older components such as resilient road wheels, rubber-rimmed return rollers and 75mm armoured turret. The turret marking, derived from the diamond used to indicate a tank on Russian military maps, has the battalion number above a two- or three-digit code identifying the brigade. (Sovfoto)

ammunition and fuel went off in successive fury. If a crewman had been foolish enough ever to have tried to recover a friend's remains from the insides of a shattered tank, he needed no imagination to sow his fear. It mattered little that tests had shown that a German 50mm KwK 38 tank round could penetrate only 54mm of armour while the crew was safely ensconced behind 75mm—they did not know that. It made no difference, anyway, if the armour was of poor quality and shattered prematurely, or if the round came within ten per cent of penetrating and knocked loose spalls of armour from the inner face of the turret, creating an action as lethal as the projectile itself. Mix these fears with the usual exhaustion of battle, and it took considerable stamina and composure to resist the atavistic urge to bolt the wretched confines of a tank in combat for the seeming freedom outside. It is not surprising that many KVs were put out of action as Yeremenko described. What is surprising is the courage of tankers like those at the Rasyeinyia crossroads and others like them, who caused many of the small delays that barred the Wehr-

macht's approach to Leningrad, Moscow and Stalingrad until the *rasputitsa* and finally the winter set in.

Rasputitsa, the season of bad roads, reaches the steppes in October as the dirt roads and farm tracks are transformed into gullies of deep clutching ooze by the freezing rains. For a few weeks, all wheeled transport waits for the onset of frost before there is any hope of moving. Coming after the frontier disasters, the encirclement of Leningrad and the surrounding of Yeremenko's forces at Bryansk, the *rasputitsa* gave the Red Army a timely lull before a hard winter of fighting. As the tanks of Panzergruppe 4 had raced up the Baltic coast to Leningrad in July, Stalin ordered the evacuation of the Kirovski Works and the related Izhorski Armour

Works to Chelyabinsk, deep in the Urals. The equipment and workers from these factories were merged with parts of the Kharkov Diesel Works and the Chelyabinsk Tractor Factory (ChTZ) to form a new complex, popularly called Tankograd (Tank City). The successful transplantation of the Kirovski works and others like it was an accomplishment as important as the victory at the gates of Moscow that winter. The newly located factories were free from the ravages of German bombers, and began to provide a stream of new tanks to rebuild the Red Army's severely drained strength. In 1941, 1,358 KVs were manufactured, of which 1,121 were KV-1s, 232 KV-2s and the remainder prototypes.

The principal aim of Kotin's SKB-2 design team became the simplification of the KV to enable maximum production. Improvements were introduced only if they did not interfere with manufacture. Already, between 1939 and the factory transference, there had been a number of different improvements to the KV series, and more were planned. It is difficult to categorise these modifications as the Soviet Army did not codify them with designations like those employed by the Wehrmacht's Waffenamt. They made scanty use of the rough model/year designation system, but with little regularity. It is often necessary to qualify these simple designations with additional details.

The standard KV-1 Model 1939 was armed with a short-barrelled L-11 76.2mm gun mounted in a low-slung pig-snout mantlet. A small pre-series batch was built without the ball-mounted hull machine gun. The L-11 gun was a stop-gap until the improved F-32 became available. The KV-1 Model 1940 was essentially similar but was armed with the F-32 in a new mantlet. In the spring of 1941, as an outcome of Kulik's contention that the Germans were up-armouring and up-arming their tanks, it was decided to begin a crash programme to up-armour the KV-1. Since the factories were not capable of handling any thicker armour it was decided to attach appliqué plates to the turret with large rivets. These were sometimes called *KV-1 s ekranami* (literally, KV with screens) and are referred to here as KV-1 Model 1940 (appliqué). These 35mm appliqué plates were riveted to the turret with narrow spacing the better to combat certain new AP rounds. They were most noticeable on the turret sides and front, though later batches had panels on the hull sides, both above and below the fender line, and had splash-strips added around the turret ring.

This attempt at up-armouring was better integrated into the design in the third production series of the Model 1940, which had an up-armoured turret. The original production turret had 90mm frontal armour and 75mm sides. The new turret armour was 95–120mm, and 95mm respectively. The up-armoured turret looked very similar to the first production batch apart from the shape under the turret overhang. On the first production batch the side armour turned in below the overhang, while on the new turret the side armour ended further back and terminated abruptly in a right angle. The side appliqué was welded rather than bolted on and consisted of two panels on either side. There was no hull appliqué below the fender line, but the frontal hull appliqué was retained as on the second production series. Towards the very end of this production series new suspension elements were used. The German invasion disrupted the supply of rubber, and as a result the rubber-rimmed return rollers were replaced with simple steel return wheels. Eventually the complicated road wheels incorporating a shock absorption system were replaced by simple one-piece cast wheels with a distinctive spoke pattern.

In July 1941 the first KV-1 Model 1941s began to appear alongisde Model 1940s. The Model 1941s were identical to the third batch Model 1940s except that they were armed with the new ZiS-5 76.2mm gun. The ZiS-5 had a longer barrel than the F-32, but its simplest distinction was a new mantlet with a hatchet-head depression on the left side for the sighting telescope. A few Model 1941s were built with the early turret, but the majority were manufactured with the up-armoured turret. Since there were still F-32s in the inventory, Model 1940 production continued simultaneously until the factory transferred to Chelyabinsk. None of the Model 1941 was built with the appliqué-style turret as far as is known.

Gradually other changes were incorporated such as replacement of the side appliqué panels with a single thicker bar of armour to protect the side of the turret race, additional splash-strips at front and rear to cover the turret ring, and replacement of the large rear tool bins with smaller containers. To speed production a cast turret was developed for the KV-1 and entered production at Chelyabinsk. It had 100mm side armour. Since facilities for the rolled plate, welded turret still existed, both cast and welded turrets were manufactured simultaneously. It was this version of the KV-1 that was sent to Bovington and the Aberdeen Proving Grounds for tests. Later in 1942 the Model 1942 was introduced. The basic change was the increase in hull side armour from 75mm to 90mm. This resulted in only minor external differences, notably the replacement of the curved rear deck by a more sharply angled shape. The Model 1942 was fitted with either the up-armoured welded turret or the cast turret. In the summer of 1942 an improved cast turret was introduced with side armour raised to 120mm. This version had the same shape as the earlier

type, but had a heavier circular armour lip around the rear MG. It should be kept in mind that many KVs underwent rebuilding after being put out of action, and this led to some retro-fit of newer features on earlier models, resulting in anomalies from the standard production models noted above. This was particularly the case with running-gear and appliqué armour. During the course of KV-1 production improved manu-facturing techniques cut the number of man-hours and material needed for each tank, and the cost per tank dropped from 635,000 roubles in 1941 to 295,000 in 1942 and 225,000 roubles in 1943.

Production details of the KV-2 somewhat paralleled those of the KV-1. The KV-2 Model 1939 was produced in very small numbers and is identifiable from the later standard production

One of the handful of KVs employed in Stalingrad, this Mod.1941 with the newer up-armoured turret is seen sup-posedly blasting German sniper positions; the turret marking is '34–18' above 'For the Homeland!' (Sovfoto)

Cutaway of KV-1 Mod.1941 (cast turret). (RAC Tank Museum)

SWITCHGEAR

AIR STARTER COCK

TRACK ADJUSTER

AIR BOTTLES

FUEL BOX

FUEL TANK

HAND

GEAR LEVER

FUEL FILLER CAP

STEERING LEVERS

CLUTCH

ACCELERATOR

HAND THROTTLE

DRIVER'S SEAT

TORSION BAR SUSPENSION

FUEL TAPS

CUT-OUT SW

ESCAPE HATCH

FUEL TANK

AERIAL ROD

AERIAL SPREADER

ADDITIONAL ARMOUR

DRIVER'S EPISCOPE

HULL L.M.G.

COMMANDER/LOADER'S PERISCOPE

PERISCOPE HEAD TRAVERSE

ELEVATION TRAVELLING LOCK

L.M.G. AMMN. RACK

CO-AXIAL L.M.G.

L.M.G. AMMN. RACK

L.M.G. AMMN. RACK

WIRELESS OPERATOR'S SEAT

L.M.G. AMMN. RACK

COMMANDER/LOADER'S SEAT

4 DOZ BOXES (2 BELOW)

FIRING PEDAL 8 76 MM

76 MM AMMN. BOXES (2 LAYERS)

2 CARTRIDGES PER BOX

FUEL TANK

MACHINE GUNNERS DETACHABLE SEAT

REAR GUNNERS TURRET RING PROTECTION

FUEL FILLER CAP

TELESCOPIC SIGHT

TURRET FUZE BOX

BATTERIES

CONDUIT FROM BASE JUNCTION

VENTILATOR

PERISCOPIC SIGHT

HORIZONTAL RING

L.M.G. IN A A MOUNTING

EPISCOPE

TURRET HATCH IN ROTATING RING

76 MM CARTRIDGES

EPISCOPE

EPISCOPE

EPISCOPE

GUNNER'S SEAT

L.M.G. AMMN. RACK

L.M.G. MAGAZINE ON STOWAGE CLIP

L.M.G. AMMN. RACK

ENGINE COMPARTMENT HATCH

18

series by the more complicated turret shape, and the exposed ribbed cheeks over the gun trunnion. The hull was the same as the KV-1 Model 1939. The standard KV-2 Model 1940 used the improved turret and eventually incorporated other small changes in hull fittings, like those on the KV-1 Model 1940, such as strap-on external fuel tanks. Production of the KV-2 was rather modest compared to the KV-1, and when the factory transfer was made in 1941 production ceased. Mainly intended as a bunker destroyer, it contributed little to the defensive battles of 1941, and was considerably more difficult to manufacture than the KV-1. It was popular in the tank regiments as a support weapon, though its massive turret was sometimes difficult to traverse if not on level ground. It was not commonly seen after the winter battles of 1941–42, due to attrition.

The KV-1 Described

The KV-1 Model 1941 (cast turret) weighed about 47 tons, and had a five-man crew: commander/loader, gunner, driver, radio-operator/ hull machine gunner and assistant driver/ mechanic. The driver sat in the centre of the hull, slightly to the right. When driving outside the combat area he could use a small hatch that could be latched up to provide direct vision. When closed down for combat he had a small slit in this visor; however, this was protected by layers of laminated glass block that were often contaminated with air bubbles and difficult to see through. Usually a small roof periscope was used, which could be traversed through a 27° arc to either side. In view of its weight and the absence of any power assistance, the KV was very difficult to steer. This accounted for the frequent complaints from engineer troops and rear service elements that KVs moving up to the front often bumped into houses, bridge sidings and any other object foolish enough to stand in their way. The tank used a multi-dry plate clutch with a sliding mesh gearbox. The transmission was undoubtedly the most troublesome mechanical component and the most frequent source of

The KV-85, in which the turret of the IS-1 was married with the hull of the KV-1S; note widened superstructure to accommodate larger turret race.

breakdowns. There had been plans to employ an improved planetary transmission, but these ended with the German invasion.

The radio operator sat to the left of the driver, and operated the hull-mounted DT 7.62mm machine gun. While radios were usually issued only to company and platoon commanders in medium and light tank companies, most KVs were radio-equipped. This was usually the older 71-TK-3 set which operated at pre-set frequencies by use of plug-in condensers—a temperamental device. The crew communicated through a TPU-4 intercom system, most of the hardware for which was mounted in front of the radio operator, who was responsible for it. The padded crash-helmets worn by the crew had a lead which plugged into a communication box near their station that controlled volume; they spoke through a throat mike. An escape hatch was provided for the driver and the radio-operator immediately above the latter, but it was only used in emergencies as it interfered with the traverse of the turret when open. When the vehicle was abandoned it was the responsibility of the radio-operator to remove the hull MG for defensive use. Often only the commander had a side arm, so the other crewmen took hand-grenades or one of the other MGs.

The turret was arranged in the traditional, clumsy 1930s fashion, without a turret basket and with the commander doubling as the loader. This arrangement dated from earlier light tanks with two-man turrets, yet when three-man turrets were introduced the Russians used the additional crewman simply to operate the rear turret MG

Rear turret interior of a KV-1 Mod.1941 (cast turret); note DT machine gun, DT drum stowage, and ten 76.2mm 'ready rounds'. The rear periscopes had canvas covers which were flipped up before use. (Ordnance Dept./National Archives)

used to keep infantry from swarming over the tank. This arrangement was not very efficient, as loading distracted the commander from his primary responsibility of directing the tank and issuing instructions to the driver and gunner. German tankers frequently commented that the Soviet tanks behaved in a very clumsy fashion, oblivious to local terrain features which could be exploited for better protection, and quite blind to many targets. Platoon-sized units showed little cohesion, and some stumbled about with little apparent regard for enemy tanks or the other tanks in their own unit. While some of these failings are attributable to poor training, much of the fault lies with the poor turret layout. This could not be remedied simply by having the third turret crewman, the assistant driver/ mechanic, take over the loading functions since the rear station where the third crewman sat had no all-around vision devices and the commander would have been virtually blind. There were plans to remedy this situation on the KV-3, but this did not materialise.

The commander was provided with a PTK periscope which was nearly the same as the PT-4-7 periscope used by the gunner but without the illuminated ballistic reticles for aiming. It could be traversed in a full circle, had 2.5 power magnification and covered an arc of 26°. In addition there was a periscope on the side and a view slit above the right side pistol port. Besides loading the main gun the commander was responsible for keeping the co-axial 7.62mm DT machine gun fed. His tasks were made ludicrously complex by the poor ammunition layout. There were ten ready rounds within easy reach, five clipped on each wall of the rear turret bustle; but once these were exhausted it was necessary to rip up the floor to get at additional rounds. In fact the floor

was made up of 44 stacked two-round containers with a rubberised pad covering them. In combat the floor soon became a ragged mess of opened containers, floor pads and spent shell casings. This clutter was the more bothersome as the assistant driver/mechanic was positioned close behind the commander/loader when the gun was in operation. Ordinarily he sat on a pad suspended from the turret race immediately behind the gun, but when the gun was in use the deflector and attached shell casing bin were folded up, filling this place. This seat was moved behind the commander, and it is not surprising that some KV crews preferred only a four-man team.

The principal functions of the assistant driver were to relieve the driver when he became exhausted using the demanding clutch-and-brake steering system, and to take care of simple maintenance when halted. During travel he was usually assigned to the roof-mounted anti-aircraft DT machine gun located on the hatch ring above his station, but sometimes the commander took this

position the better to direct the vehicle. During combat he was assigned to the rear turret MG to keep infantry off the tank. The German infantry had a number of anti-tank mines which could disable a KV if properly positioned, and special care was needed when fighting in towns or wooded areas where infantry could approach unseen.

The gunner sat in the left front corner of the turret opposite the commander. He was provided with two sighting instruments for the gun, a PT-4-7 periscope with illuminated reticles, and a 2.5 power TMFD direct telescopic sight which was articulated with the gun's elevation. Range-finding was of the simple stadiametric variety:

One of the frequent presentation ceremonies, at which local dignitaries would hand over tanks paid for by the contributions of local communities; here, a citizens' group in Moscow hands over a company of KV-1s Mod.1942 to their crews, the turrets inscribed *'Dzerzhinyets'*. The up-armoured hull of this variant can be identified by the sharp angles of the previously rounded rear engine deck. The turrets are, from left to right: up-armoured cast, standard cast, standard cast, and up-armoured welded. (Sovfoto)

a target was put in the cross hairs, and depending how large the enemy tank appeared against the fine stadia lines, a range could be readily estimated. There were adjustments provided for one HE and two AP rounds. Ranging was reasonably quick and simple, and effective at close ranges. The early versions of the KV were provided with a clinometer for indirect artillery firing but this had been deleted by the Model 1941. The gunner elevated the gun with his right arm, and could traverse the turret manually with his left arm or by using electric traverse. The electric traverse had three speeds, the fastest traversing 360° in 70 seconds, the slowest (for fine adjustments) in two minutes.

The KV-1 was powered by the same V-2 diesel engine as was used on the T-34, providing 600 horsepower. The early versions had a maximum road speed of 35km/h (22mph), but on the up-armoured Model 1942 this dropped to 28km/h (17mph). The KV's torsion bar suspension gave it a better ride than the spring suspension of the T-34. Wide tracks offered far better flotation on soft soil or snow than the narrow tracks of contemporary German tanks. After the experiences in Finland a number of features had been added to Soviet tanks to improve cold-weather performance, particularly in respect of cold starting and lubricants. British and US evaluations of the KV found the design to be simple and robust. The finish was often poor, though not on moving parts where fit was important, and the quality of armour was found to be excellent. It is worth noting that when a KV at Aberdeen Proving Grounds was examined long after the war it was found that despite being outside, exposed to the elements, without maintenance, for all of 35 years, the turret traverse still worked easily.

Revival of the Soviet Tank Force

Following the bloody débâcle of summer 1941 and the dogged resistance before Moscow and Leningrad in winter 1941–42, efforts began to rejuvenate the Soviet tank force. The 'tank division' establishments had faded away through attrition. Smaller units were formed in their place: 'tank brigades' for independent operations, and 'regiments' (battalions) for support of infantry and cavalry divisions. The August 1941 tank brigade establishment was for 93 tanks: 22 T-34s, seven KVs and 64 of whatever kind of light tank was available. In view of the huge losses these were wildly optimistic figures, and in September the total was reduced to 67 including seven KVs. The battalion-sized infantry-support regiments had 29 tanks but no KVs, which were being reserved for the tank brigades; this led to an outcry from divisional commanders who prized its near-invulnerability. The transfer of factories to the Urals caused a temporary drought in armour equipment, so that by February 1942 tank brigade strength reached its nadir at a mere 27 tanks of which ten were supposed to be KVs. This soon improved; the nominal brigade strength in the spring was 46 tanks with ten KVs. By this time the tank brigades were divided into two battalions, each with a light, a medium and a heavy company; the latter consisted of two platoons of two KVs each and a company commander's KV. Heavy companies usually led

counter-attacks due to their excellent armour.

Although Soviet tankers had a lot to learn from their more experienced adversaries, a number of units had accumulated a good deal of skill in the hard winter fighting, and gave the Germans a rough time in the defensive battles of summer 1942. An example was the encounter between two Soviet tank brigades and the 11th and 19th Panzer Divisions during the German drive against Kolsovo on the Bryansk Front in July 1942. The German attack was into a natural pocket formed by woods to the west, the Vitebsk River to the north and the Resseta River to the east; the pocket was about ten miles wide, with the town of Kolsovo in the north below the river. 19th Panzer advanced along the edge of woods while 11th Panzer moved up the river. The initial attack was launched against a series of entrenched

KV-1S variants of a heavy tank regiment, presented in the name of a delegation from the Far North: the turret inscription is 'Sovyetskikh Polyarnik', polyarnik being the term for Russians living in the Arctic regions. The KV-1S was a retrograde step in the tank's evolution, sacrificing armour for performance; note cupola, smaller and better-shaped turret and more sharply angled rear hull. (Sovfoto)

anti-tank guns and infantry. The guns took a heavy toll before the Germans realised that the gun positions they were firing against were dummies mounted on farm carts, and that the real guns were dug in so that only their barrels showed. Once through this defensive belt 19th Panzer got entangled with two companies of BTs which darted in and out of the woods. As the 19th tried to rout out the harassing light tanks, 11th Panzer became the victim of hit-and-run attacks by a T-34 company using uneven ground for cover. The outnumbered Soviets refused an engagement which would have pitted them against a better-equipped foe. The T-34s finally lured some of 11th Panzer's tanks into hilly terrain, where they were ambushed by dug-in KVs. The Germans had to call in air support before they could locate and finally penetrate these defenders. As they approached Kolsovo later in the day, the 11th Panzer Division again suffered hit-and-run raids by T-34s. While staging a fighting withdrawal the T-34s lured the German tanks on through the town, where they were struck on their north flank by entrenched anti-tank guns, and from their rear and side by another Soviet tank brigade. A fierce battle ensued for Kolsovo, forcing 11th Panzer to throw in its reserves to gain a firm grip on the town.

This encounter north of Rechitsa in July 1942 offers a classic example of skilful feint and ambush by an outnumbered force. The two Soviet brigades, outnumbered over three to one, successfully delayed the advance of two Panzer divisions, permitting the Red Army to re-establish its defensive positions north of the river, while exacting disproportionate losses in the process. It is also interesting to note that in the encounter the KVs were used in a static rôle.

By 1942 Soviet brigade commanders were having difficulties using their assortment of tanks in a cohesive fashion. The continued up-armouring of the KV diminished its effective cross-country speed so much that it could not keep up with the fleet T-34s and T-60 light tanks. While the KV had been universally popular in 1941 because of its armour advantages, by 1942 the Germans were introducing new guns and ammunition to deal with it, and its vices were becoming more evident. In June 1942, for example, Lt.Col.

Strogiy, who commanded a tank brigade fighting on the Kerch peninsula, reported to STAVKA that his KVs had been penetrated by a new German round using the shaped-charge principle. Several of the top Soviet tank commanders were questioned about their views on Soviet armoured equipment by STAVKA.

Gen. Pavel Rotmistrov, who began the war as a colonel commanding the 8th Tank Bde. and ended the war in charge of the Soviet armoured forces, replied: 'The difficulty is that while there isn't much difference in speed between the light [T-60] and medium [T-34] on the roads, when moving cross-country the light tanks are quickly left behind. The heavy tank [KV] is already behind and often crushed local bridges which cut off units following behind. Under battlefield conditions, that too often meant that the T-34 alone arrived; the light tanks had difficulty fighting the German tanks anyway and the KVs were still delayed in the rear. It was also difficult to command these companies as they sometimes were equipped with different types of radios or none at all.'

Rotmistrov's opinions were not universally shared, and he sent a team of engineers from Tankograd to visit one of his battalions attached to the 7th Tank Corps commanded by Col. I. A. Vovochenko. The crews belittled the complaints, and an old-timer who had driven tractors at an agricultural station before the war quipped 'After running those damn old tractors, well the KV . . . that's class!'

The problem of the slow KVs not being able to keep up with the other tanks was most seriously felt in the newly raised 'tank corps'. The tank corps were in fact divisional-sized formations with two tank brigades and a brigade of motorised infantry plus support elements. Until a technical solution could be developed it was decided to pull most of the KVs out of the mixed tank brigades and form them into independent heavy tank regiments for use by army commanders in assault and infantry support missions; formed in October 1942 these units had 21 KV-1s each, divided into four platoons. But clearly design improvements were desperately needed.

The SKB-2 design team was in a quandary. On the one hand the troops in the field wanted a

1. T-35 Model 1935, 5th Ind. Heavy Tk. Bde.; Moscow, 1938

2. KV-1 Model 1940 (up-armoured turret); Leningrad, 1941

1. KV-1 Model 1941 (up-armoured turret), 118th Ind. Tk. Bn.;
   Leningrad, 1942

2. KV-1 Model 1941 (initial turret); Western Front, 1941

1. KV-1 Model 1940 (appliqué), Lt. I. Pilyayef; September 1941

2. KV-1 Model 1941 (up-armoured turret), 12th Tk. Regt.,
1st Moscow Motor Rifle Div.; August 1942

C

1. KV-1 Model 1941 (cast turret); Kursk salient, June 1943

НЕВСКИИ

2. KV-1 Model 1941 (cast turret); South-West Front, summer 1942

1. KV-1S, 121st Tk. Bde.; Stalingrad, January 1943

2. KV-1 Model 1942 (up-armoured cast turrent), 3rd Coy.,
1st Tk. Bde., Finnish 1st Armd.Div., Ihantala, August 1944

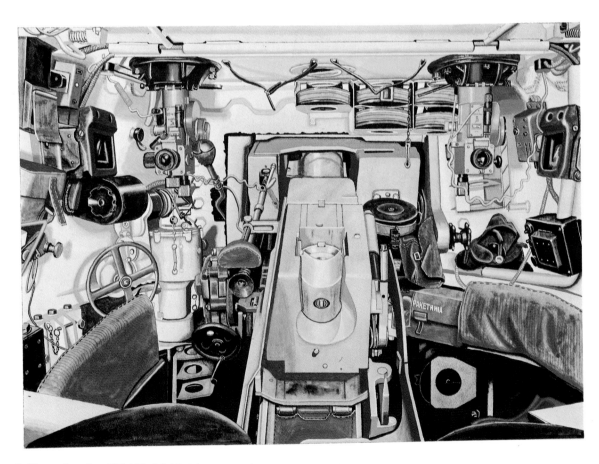

БОЯВАЯ ПОДРУГА

1. IS-2m, 85th Heavy Tk. Regt.; Berlin, 1945

2. Turret interior, KV-1 Model 1941 (cast turret);
   see Plates copy for key

F

1. IS-2m, Czechoslavak 1st Tk. Bde., Prague, 1945

2. IS-2m, Polish 4th Ind. Heavy Tk. Regt.; Germany, 1945

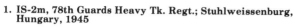
1. IS-2m, 78th Guards Heavy Tk. Regt.; Stuhlweissenburg, Hungary, 1945

2. IS-3M, Egyptian 4th Armoured Div.; Cairo, 1967

faster, heavier tank. They also wanted the thick armour retained or improved in view of the appearance of new German tank guns and ammunition such as the shaped-charge rounds and the tungsten-cored AP rounds. On the other hand the industrial representatives at the GKO (Central Defence Committee, headed by Stalin) were reluctant to introduce a new, more powerful engine since it would badly upset production at a time when tanks were desperately needed on the Stalingrad front.

The design team had not been idle. While much of their effort had been directed towards manufacturing improvements, a number of new design initiatives had been undertaken. In many respects, the KV-3 would have been the ideal solution if it had entered production in 1942 as planned; however, it required a new powerplant. One example of these new designs to reach production was the KV-8 flamethrower tank, which saw service in small numbers.

A stopgap solution was the KV-1S (s: *skorostnyi* = speedy), a lightened version of the KV-1 Model 1942 of which 1,370 were built between August 1942 and April 1943. A smaller, thinner turret of better ballistic shape featured an improved layout, the commander being relieved of his rôle as loader and given an all-round vision cupola behind the gunner's station. Other changes were 75mm hull armour, reduced appliqué armour, light-weight wheels, a streamlined engine deck and new periscopes. The KV-1S was rushed to the new independent heavy tank regiments; some were also used by regular tank brigades, due to their improved speed. Among the first units so equipped were those earmarked for the Stalingrad counter-offensive; the best-known of these was the 121st Tank Bde. of the 62nd Army, later granted the title 27th Guards Tank Bde. for its performance in that campaign.

The Kotin team's approach was not universally popular among tankers; many expected to encounter new German designs which would require better Soviet tank armament. At a meeting with Stalin in September 1942 Gen. M. E. Katukov—who commanded the first Soviet tank brigade to be granted the 'Guards' title, for service at Mtensk before Moscow in October 1941[1]—was asked for

[1] See Vanguard No. 14, *The T-34 Tank.*

The SU-152 prototype, built in only 25 days in response to the threat of the German Tiger E tank.

his opinion of the quality of Soviet tanks, and replied: 'The T-34 fulfills all our hopes and has proven itself in combat. But the KV heavy tank . . . the soldiers don't like it. . . . It is very heavy and clumsy and not very agile. It surmounts obstacles with great difficulty. It often damages bridges and becomes involved in other accidents. More to the point, it is equipped with the same 76mm gun as the T-34. This raises the question, to what extent is it superior to the T-34? If the KV had a more potent gun or one of greater calibre, then it might be possible to excuse its weight and other shortcomings.'

Katukov's views were remarkably prescient: in January 1943 the Red Army captured a new Tiger E near Leningrad. Heavily armoured and armed with a derivative of the 88mm Flak gun, it could not be penetrated by the Soviet 76.2mm gun of the T-34, KV-1S and SU-76 Suka tank destroyer. At Kursk the following July the Soviets would encounter the Panther, well armoured and better armed than any Soviet tank. Clearly, the technical advantage enjoyed by the Soviets since June 1941 was about to disappear.[2]

Various heavy tank designs were under way under the designation KV-13, but none were sufficiently developed; as a temporary antidote to the Tiger the GKO therefore ordered on 4 January 1943 that the SKB-2 team begin urgent work on a heavy SP gun. Kotin and L. Troyanov began work on two projects. The KV-12s planned 203mm howitzer lacked the range to engage the '88'; but the ML-20 152mm gun-howitzer of the

[2] See Vanguard No. 20, *The Tiger Tanks*, and 21, *The PzKpfw V Panther.*

The KV-13T was one of a series of experimental designs which evaluated new heavy tank components; the hull armour layout later used on the IS-1 can be seen on this prototype.

KV-14 was more promising. The prototype—a simple fixed superstructure on a KV-1S chassis—was built in only 25 days; trials went smoothly, and on 4 February the GKO ordered Red Army adoption of the design as the SU-152 (SU: *Samokhodnaya Ustanovka* = self-propelled mount). Planned KV-1S construction was reduced in favour of the new tank destroyer, and assembly of the first SU-152 began on 1 March 1943.

The Kursk-Orel battles of summer 1943 marked the swansong of the KVs; of 3,400 Soviet tanks on the Central Front, only 205 were 'heavies', and of these at least one regiment were Lend-Lease Churchills. Production of heavy tanks dropped sharply in 1943—452 KV-1Ss were built that year, compared to 2,553 in 1942, an obvious acknowledgement of the tank's shortcomings. The experience of the 2nd Bn., 181st Tank Bde., 18th Tank Corps near Petrovka illustrates the changed fortunes of the KV. Capt. P. Skrypin's

battalion attacked a Panzer unit in hilly terrain, but was badly torn up by the longer-range guns of the static Tigers. Ordering his KV-1S forward on an evasive course in a successful attempt to rally his shaken unit, Skrypin hit one Tiger at least three times. His KV was then hit twice, killing the loader and badly wounding Skrypin, who was dragged from the smouldering wreck by the driver and operator while the gunner remained at his post. The 76.2mm gun was unable to cripple an approaching Tiger, however, and the gunner died from a third '88' hit. To protect Skrypin where he lay wounded in a shellhole, the driver returned to the burning KV and rammed the Tiger, whereupon the ammunition stowage exploded with shattering effect.

The SU-152 fared better at Kursk. A heavy SP regiment with 12 guns—later raised to its full strength of 21—was committed by High Command Reserve; in three weeks of combat it claimed 12 Tigers and seven Elefants, giving rise to the SU-152's unofficial nickname of *Zvierboy*—Animal Hunter!

The inadequacy of the 76.2mm ZiS-5 gun was now painfully obvious; at Kursk many Soviet

tanks were gutted by Tiger and Panther units at over 1,000 metres, and the key engagement at Prokhorovka was won only be getting to point-blank range—sometimes only 300m—by clever use of terrain.

For the accelerated development of a new heavy tank the SKB-2 team was split. The Factory No. 100 team lead by Kotin came up with a radically new vehicle dubbed the 'IS' (IS: *Iosef Stalin*—the transliteration 'JS' is incorrect). A prototype IS-1, or IS-85, was shown to Stalin in August 1943. It had a thickly-armoured, large diameter turret mounting the new D-5T 85mm gun designed by the Petrov bureau; an uprated version of the same engine as the KV and T-34; and a new planetary transmission which cured the problems suffered by the KV. The running gear was similar to that of the KV, but the hull was radically redesigned, incorporating the cast front evolved during the KV-13 programme. The improved turret layout of the KV-1S was retained, but the fifth crewman (the radio operator) was eliminated to save space.

Since the IS-1 would not be ready for quantity production for some months, while facilities for

casting the new turret were already available, 130 hybrids were built as a stopgap measure in September/October 1943 by mating the IS-1 turret with the KV-1S hull. This 'KV-85' had hull fillets to widen the turret race, and related internal changes; the hull MG was discarded from the final production batch. Attrition during the winter fighting of 1943 absorbed most of these tanks.

The use of the 85mm gun in the IS-1 proved shortsighted, and although some were built at Chelyabinsk with this weapon they were subsequently re-armed before issue. Two larger guns were considered. The IS-100 project mounted the BS-3 100mm gun, with good armour penetration and a high rate of fire; while the IS-122's A19 122mm weapon fired a more effective HE round. This general-purpose capability, and better production facilities, tipped the scale. In November 1943 the IS-122 was demonstrated at the Kubinka

Proving Grounds near Moscow. The first round at 1,500m ripped through the thick frontal armour of a captured Panther, and blasted out through the rear hull armour! The enthusiastic GKO ruled in favour of Red Army acceptance, under the designation IS-2. Production began in December, and 103 IS-1s and IS-2s were built by the end of 1943. During the slight delay while a more effective muzzle brake was produced the initial IS-1s were re-armed with the 122mm gun. The following April a new assembly hall at Tankograd was authorised to speed up production. Two SP derivatives were also initiated; the ISU-122 and ISU-152 were armed with the A-19 122mm gun and the ML-20 152mm gun-howitzer respectively, in fixed superstructures.

Careful design of hull and turret armour layout gave greater protection for about the same weight as the KV-1 Model 1942: from 90 to 120mm at the bow, and from 100 to 160mm on the turret front and sides. The IS-2 was invulnerable to the

standard 88mm AP round at ranges over 1,000m when fired against the frontal quadrant, and the turret front armour could only be penetrated by the more effective PzGr. 40 tungsten-carbide round at about 500m. The 122mm gun offered 2.7 times more kinetic energy on impact than the 85mm gun, and 3.5 times more than the old 76.2mm weapon. Firing the BR-471N AP/HE round it could penetrate 160mm of armour at 1,000m, and the impact of this 25kg round was devastating. The only shortcoming was the rate of fire, slowed to about two or three rounds per minute by the use of a two-piece round with separate brass cartridge; and only 28 rounds were carried. A partial remedy adopted on 1944 production models was the improved D-25T gun, which had a handier drop-breech instead of the conventional artillery screw-breech.

The first IS-2s were issued to Guards Heavy Tank Regiments early in 1944; these units had four companies of five tanks each, two recovery tanks (usually turretless KVs), three APCs (Universal Carriers or White M3A1 Scout Cars), one BA-64 armoured car, and 48 assorted trucks. The first to see action was the 11th Guards Independent Heavy Tank Bde. commanded by Col. Tsiganov, which saw combat around Terno-

The only heavy tank supplied to Russia through Lend-Lease was the Churchill; they were used when available, but their slow speed and poor armament were unpopular. This Mk III in winter whitewash served with a Guards heavy tank regiment in winter 1943–44; the Guards insignia is painted on each side of the turret front, and the number '61' in red high on the turret side. (Sovfoto)

Majestic view of two IS-2s of a heavy tank regiment serving with 2nd Ukrainian Front in Hungary in December 1944. Evident here is the KV-13-style hull front with the opening driver's visor, a distinctive feature of early production models. (Sovfoto)

pol late in the Korsun-Shevchenkovsky Pocket battle. Among its opponents were the Tigers of sPzAbt. 503. As the first Soviet tank which could take on Tigers and Panthers at long ranges and knock them out with ease, the IS-2 proved immediately popular with its crews. Even at ranges too great for the 122mm round to penetrate, the concussion of impact was often enough to damage the turret race or otherwise disable the target. It is often forgotten when comparing the IS-2 with the German heavy tanks that it was in fact in the same weight and size class as the Panther medium, and considerably lighter than the Tiger. Its qualities were not lost on its opponents. Generalleutnant Hasso von Manteuffel, commanding the crack 'Grossdeutschland' Panzer Division, recounts his unit's first encounter with the IS-2:

'Our Tigers met the Stalins for the first time . . . in May 1944 in Romania during the battle for Targul Frumos. . . . Not having seen this type before, our Tigers opened fire from 3,000m, and the crews noted that the 88mm rounds ricocheted off the armour ! . . . Some Tigers crept up to

within 1,800m, where they succeeded in knocking out two Stalins, while three more attempted to set up ambushes to destroy the Russian vehicles from the rear . . . This encounter was shocking, as previously our 88mm gun had destroyed Russian tanks with direct hits at maximum ranges without difficulty. Now the Tiger crews could destroy the enemy tanks only with the greatest difficulty and suffering heavy losses.'

Intended mainly for use against German heavy tanks at long ranges, and the suppression of AT guns and reinforced emplacements, the IS-2 regiments were initially assigned to Armies to add shock value to selected assaults, usually operating in conjunction with a T-34 brigade. Some 300–500m behind the initial wave of T-34s came the Stalins, on a front of 1,000–1,500m; they provided long-range supporting fire, passing

29

through the T-34s to spearhead the attack if a particularly difficult position was encountered. A regiment of ISU-122s or ISU-152s was sometimes added in a third wave for even greater firepower. The IS-2 was always supposed to be accompanied into action by a squad of tank-riders, to give protection against German tank-killer teams with rocket launchers. The success of the IS-2 at Korsun and in similar engagements led the GKO to increase production to allow allotment of one heavy regiment to each tank corps.

In spring 1944 the improved IS-2m was introduced at Tankograd (m: *modifikatsirovanny* = modified). This had an improved bow casting,

a wider mantlet, and the MK-4 periscopic gunner's sight instead of the old PT-4-17 'gumdrop' sight. Production of IS-2s totalled 2,250 in 1944 and 1,150 in January–May 1945. This allowed formation of special assault units, the Guards Independent Heavy Tank Brigades, each with three regiments of IS-2s, totalling 65 tanks. Among the first of these was the 30th Guards Vyborgska Independent Tank Bde.; originally the 61st Light Tank Bde., its T-60s had been badly mauled by Tigers of sPzAbt.502 at Leningrad in winter 1942–43, and it had gone on to fight with distinction in T-34s on the same front (see Vanguard No. 14, *The T-34 Tank*). Re-organised with IS-2s at Tula in December

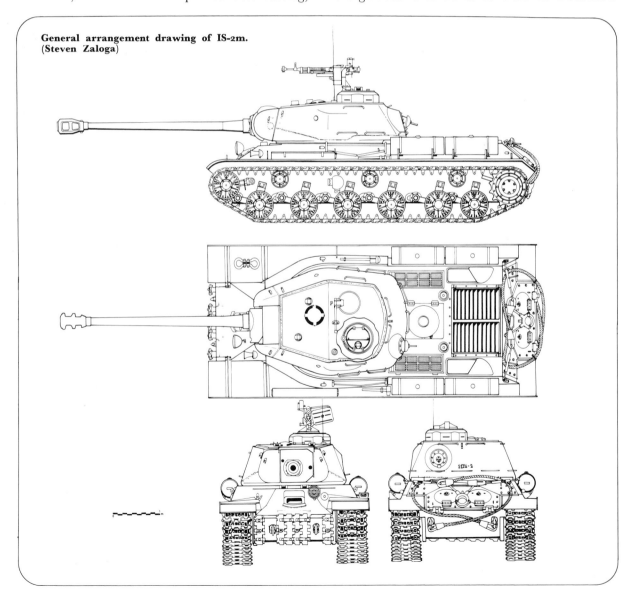

General arrangement drawing of IS-2m.
(Steven Zaloga)

1944, it again fought sPzAbt.502—though now on more equal terms—on the Narva River in Poland. The IS-2 units played a very important part in the fighting in Germany and Czechoslovakia in 1945.

Cheaper and simpler to build than the IS-2, the SP derivatives were produced in slightly larger numbers; 4,075 ISU-122s and ISU-152s were built by the end of the war. With firepower advantages over the tank version at close ranges, the ISU-152 was mainly employed in the direct fire rôle, much like a tank; and of 53 heavy SP regiments raised, many were based on tank units. The most famous was the 399th Guards Proskurovsky Heavy SP Gun Regt. im. Kotovsky, a unit which traced its lineage back to the 1st Armoured Car Detachment formed at Petersburg in 1917. As the 61st Guards Heavy Tank Regt. this unit distinguished itself at Kharkov. Receiving ISU-122s in February 1944, its heaviest fighting came that April at Nezvisko near the Romanian border, where it destroyed 70 Panzers in two days. The success of the SPs led to the formation of special Guards Heavy SP Brigades in March 1945, each with 65 ISUs and three SU-76s organised in the same way as a tank brigade. They played an important rôle in the fight for Berlin.

Following the decision to proceed with the IS-2, the unsuccessful Dukhov team was ordered to work on a more effective armour layout for the IS-2. The prototype IS-3, completed in November 1944, was internally nearly identical (though with a constant mesh instead of sliding gear transmission), but externally of new and superior ballistic shape. After tests, production was authorised alongside the closely related IS-2, and some 350 were built before VE-Day. First issued to heavy tank regiments at the time of the battle of Berlin, they saw little if any combat. One of the first units to receive the 'Shchuka', or 'Pike'—from its sharply pointed prow—was the 4th Guards Kantemirovets Tank Corps. Seen by Western observers in Berlin on 7 September 1945, when a 2nd Guards Army unit drove 52 of them past the stands as part of the Victory in the Pacific parade, they made a lingering impression. Its sleek cast turret shape was the forerunner of many post-war designs on both sides of the Iron Curtain.

One KV regiment soldiered on beside a number of IS-2 units in the 1945 Far East campaign

31

against Japan. Several Soviet-allied armies were issued with the 'heavies'. The Polish People's Army (LWP) used some KVs for training, and its first heavy tank unit, the 4th Independent Heavy Tank Regt. (4 spczc) saw action with IS-2s in Pomerania in January 1945; by VE-Day it had accounted for 31 armoured vehicles and 76 guns for a loss of 14 tanks destroyed and four damaged. The 5th Regt. went into action in the last weeks of the war in Prague and Berlin; and the 6th and 7th were being formed as the war ended. The LWP also included the 25th SP Arty. Regt. with 21 ISU-122s, and the 13th SP Arty. Regt. with nine ISU-152s and SU-85s. The Czech 1st Tank Bde. had a small number of IS-2s in April 1945, but these saw no major combat.

IS-3M captured from the Egyptian Army on parade in Israel in 1968, showing to perfection the low, sleek lines of this tank. This version incorporated a new engine and many detail improvements over the 1945 production model, and is sometimes wrongly identified as the IS-4. (IDF)

Post-War Service

The advent of the IS-3 ended IS-2 production. A few IS-2s were exported to China and Cuba. In the 1950s the remaining tanks were remanufactured to IS-2M configuration, with internal improvements, a new V-54K-IS engine and new stowage bins. Similar modification produced the IS-3M. Although a number of experimental prototypes were based on the IS-2 and -3, only the IS-4 was built in any numbers—about 200 examples in 1945; this had 250mm turret armour, and explored the use of novel oscillating turrets. In 1952 a heavily modernised derivative of IS-3, designated IS-10, was accepted for quantity production. It had a lengthened hull, an extra pair of road wheels, a new and more heavily armoured turret, new external stowage bins, and a fume extractor on the gun. Due to Stalin's

death in 1953 it was redesignated T-10 when it entered service in that year. It was quickly followed by an improved T-10M version in 1957, externally distinguishable by the KPV 14.5mm MG replacing the usual DShK on the turret roof, and the five-baffle muzzle brake. Late models had large turret stowage bins. The T-10M was not exported in large numbers, contrary to some reports.

Total heavy tank production after 1945 is not known, though believed to be of the order of 6,000. As late as 1978 some 3,000 remained on the Red Army inventory with Category 3 and reserve units and in reserve stockpiles. The heavy tank passed into history in the late 1950s, with the realisation by Soviet designers that newer NATO tank guns such as the 105mm L7 could penetrate any practical armour thickness at normal ranges; and that such new Soviet guns as the 115mm U5-T under development for the T-62 tank were far superior to the 122mm weapon, and could penetrate any NATO tank without the need for a special heavy tank to give long-range support. The distinctions 'heavy' and 'medium' are now

This T-10M draws wary glances from Czech civilians in Prague during the August 1968 invasion; note white air identification crosses used once more. The multi-baffle muzzle brake is the main distinguishing feature between the T-10M and earlier T-10. (Simon Dunstan)

irrelevant, and both rôles are embraced by the new notion of the 'main battle tank'. Western overestimation of the potential of the Soviet 'heavies' led to such reciprocal monstrosities as the British Conqueror and American M103, however; in the 1950s analysts did not appreciate the compromises that allowed Russia to install such heavy, sleek armour on a relatively small vehicle. Sluggish and under-powered, the Stalins had indifferent armament, rudimentary fire controls (particularly for long-range engagements), and were unbearably cramped; the two-piece ammunition was vulnerable to internal fires, and reduced the rate of firing. These drawbacks became evident in the Middle East war of 1967. The Egyptian Army had a regiment of IS-3Ms with the 7th Inf. Div. at Rafah, and the 125th Tank Bde. of the 6th Mechanised Div. near

Kuntilla. During the fighting Egypt lost 73 IS-3Ms, which proved easy prey for the M48 and Centurion, especially at long range. At least one regiment of obsolete IS-3s was still in Egyptian service in 1973. Russia's reported T-70 heavy design does not seem to have progressed beyond prototype stage.

The Plates

A1: T-35 Model 1935, 5th Independent Heavy Tank Bde.; Moscow, 1938

Coloured turret bands often distinguished battalions within Soviet brigades in the 1930s. In the 5th, red and white identified Shtemenko's Training Bn. in Moscow, and white the second battalion; these were painted on all five turrets. The red star appeared on both hull sides. The patch shows the stripes used on the main turrets only of some T-35s of the 34th Tank Div. in 1941; painted above the side vision slits, they were about 45cm long.

IS-2m unit passing through a birch forest outside Berlin, May 1945; interestingly, they do not carry the white air recognition markings ordered at this period. The new front hull of the IS-2m is clearly seen here. Note small white star painted on right side of mantlet, as viewed. (Sovfoto)

A2: KV-1 Model 1940 (up-armoured turret); Leningrad, 1941

Repaired at one of the Leningrad tank centres, this KV was gaudily decorated with the slogan 'We Defend the Conquests of October'—referring to the Revolution of October 1917. See photo elsewhere in this book for slightly differing presentation on the other side of the turret.

B1: KV-1 Model 1941 (up-armoured turret), 118th Ind. Tank Bn.; Leningrad, 1942

Cobbled together at Leningrad's 27th Remzavod (Tank Repair Centre), this tank bears the large slogan 'For Leningrad' above another in smaller script: 'From the Leningrad Women to the Front'. This refers to the fact that, like many tank factory workers of the period, the brigade which repaired this KV were women.

The Soviets did not follow a standard tactical numbering system on tanks. The '716' could

Polish IS-2m of the 4th Independent Heavy Tank Regt. demonstrating that what was good enough for Julius Caesar is good enough for the Red Army—crossing a blown bridge by the classic method of fascine fill. It has jettisoned external fuel tanks, and has lost the fifth roadwheel in a mine explosion. See Plate G2.

indicate 6th tank, 1st Platoon, '7' being the spurious assigned company number; but as KV platoons did not exceed five tanks, this is probably not the case. A system occasionally employed was to use the last two or three digits of the manufacturer's serial number. Battalion records were kept in this way, and many Soviet unit histories refer to individual tanks by serial rather than tactical numbers. The paint finish of this tank is the usual winter whitewash over Soviet dark green.

B2: KV-1 Model 1941; Western Front, 1941

This KV of an unidentified unit has the name 'Shchortz', honouring a Bolshevik general of the

35

IS-2m unit photographed in the streets of Berlin, 1 May 1945. The crews appear to wear waist-length leather jackets and the black cloth summer-issue tank helmets over khaki overalls tucked into knee-boots. Note air recognition band on turret of further tank. (Sovfoto)

Russian Civil War. The very unusual tactical number, combining '33' with the Cyrillic letter 'N', is unexplained.

C1: KV-1 Model 1940 (appliqué) of Lt. I. Pilyayef; September 1941

For a presentation ceremony this tank bore the large chalked slogan 'Victory Will Be Ours' on both sides.

C2: KV-1 Model 1941 (up-armoured turret), 12th Tank Regt., 1st Moscow Motor Rifle Div.; August 1942

This is the famous *'Bezposhadni'*—'Merciless'—commanded by Lt. Pavel Khoroshilov. It was 'subscribed for' by Moscow's artists, poets and dancers during 1942. During the course of

fighting from 1942 to winter 1943–44 it was credited with 12 Panzers, three artillery pieces, seven mortars, four heavy MGs, seven armoured cars, four SP anti-tank guns, ten trucks, five motorcycles, a staff bus and a supply dump. These were noted by painting small white stars below the name on the rear turret sides, as inset. Forward of these was a poem by M. Kupriyanof: 'Storming through fire goes/ Our KV heavy tank/ From the heartland it rolls/ To smash the Nazi flank./ Crewed by heroic men/ Never showing fear/ As they carry out commands/ Of their homeland dear.'

D1: KV-1 Model 1941 (cast turret); Battle of Kursk, 1943

The slogan is 'Twenty-Fifth of October'—the date of the 1917 Revolution according to the old-style Julian calendar; in the West the Gregorian calendar gives the date as 7 November.

D2: KV-1 Model 1941 (cast turret); South-West Front, summer 1942

This KV carries the name '*Nevskii*', after the legendary Prince Alexander Nevskii who defeated the Teutonic Knights in the 13th century. Eisenstein's famous film popularised this historical character, and the name appeared on many tanks and aircraft. Inset is the unidentified unit insignia. This tank is believed to have served in one of the early Tank Corps; the '3' probably indicates the brigade and the '2' the battalion within the brigade. This marking was repeated centrally on the upper rear hull plate.

E1: KV-1S, 121st Tank Bde.; Stalingrad, January 1943

The tanks of this brigade were purchased by contributions from farmers of the Chelyabinsk area near the Tankograd factory complex; the slogan reads 'Chelyabinski Farmers'. From accounts of this brigade in action it seems that at some stage the tanks had two-digit tactical numbers painted on the turret sides; tank No. 18

After bitter fighting an IS-2m of the 85th Heavy Tank Regt. rests before the captured Brandenburg Gate in Berlin; see Plate F1. (Sovfoto)

particularly distinguished itself during the Stalingrad counter-offensive.

E2: KV-1 Model 1942 (up-armoured cast turret), 3rd Coy., 1st Tank Bde., Finnish 1st Armoured Div.; Ihantala, August 1944

The Finns used a handful of captured KV-1s in 1944, camouflaged in a pattern of mid-grey and dark brown over Soviet dark green. The national *hakaristi* insignia in black trimmed with white was carried on both turret sides, the centre of the upper rear hull, the turret hatch and the left side of the turret rear. The vehicle serial was painted on the hull front. The blue and white national flag was lodged into a small crevice at the forward edge of the turret. Note the mixture of wheel types, and the use of old-style roadwheels.

F1: IS-2m, 85th Heavy Tank Regt.; Berlin, 1945
This colourful IS-2m fought near the Reichstag with 4th Guards Tank Army. On the turret rear was painted the name '*Boyeva Podruga*'—roughly, 'Friend in Battle'—after the similarly-named T-34 crewed by the only woman tanker to win the Heroine of the Soviet Union decoration, Sgt. M. V. Oktyabr'skaya (see Plate B2 and text, Vanguard No. 14, *The T-34 Tank*). The white turret bands and roof cross were adopted by Soviet armour in April 1945 in agreement with the RAF and USAAF, to prevent roving Allied fighter-bombers shooting-up friendly tanks;

British and US tanks were supposed to be identified by bright orange panels. In May 1945 the markings illustrated were ordered changed to a large white triangle on turret roof and sides, when German crews were reported to be copying the Soviet markings, but few Soviet units bothered

ISU-122 in the streets of Gdansk in April 1945; the inscription behind the number '76' on the side is unfortunately indistinct. The ISU-122 and -152 were virtually identical apart from the gun, though the latter can be distinguished by its multi-baffle muzzle brake. The ISU-122S used the same brake as the IS-2 tank. (Sovfoto)

to make the change. The unit insignia was a white boar on a red star. The turret numbers follow Soviet 1944 practices and indicate 4th tank, 3rd Company, the first '4' being the number assigned to this regiment.

F2: Turret interior, KV-1 Model 1941 (cast turret); see accompanying key:

1 Gunner's side periscope
2   ,,   TPU communication box
3   ,,   viewport
4   ,,   pistol port handle
5 Turret traverse motor
6 Turret traverse wheel
7 Gun elevation wheel
8 Gunner's PT-4-7 periscopic sight
9   ,,   TMFD telescopic gun sight
10   ,,   protective rib pad
11 76.2mm F-34 tank gun
12 Co-axial DT 7.62mm MG
13 Gun trunnion and mount
14 DT drum stowage racks
15 Casing catch-bag
16 Commander's PTK sight
17   ,,   TPU communication box
18 Breech opening lever
19 Commander's helmet, w.TPU leads
20   ,,   protective rib pad
21 Flare pistol box
22 Commander's viewport

G1: IS-2m, Czechoslovak 1st Tank Bde.; Prague 1945

Finished in standard Soviet green, this tank carries the Czechoslovak roundel on the turret, and has a flag lodged in a gap near the upper mantlet cover at the right front edge of the turret.

G2: IS-2m, Polish 4th Independent Heavy Tank Regt.; Germany, 1945

This tank carries the white turret striping and roof cross illustrated on Plate F1. Numbers indicate the 4th tank of the 3rd company. The national insignia, a white Piast-style eagle, is carried on a red diamond. Note missing fifth roadwheel on right side and spare suspension arm lashed to right front fender.

Rare photo purportedly showing an IS-3 of the 4th Guards Kantemirovetz Tank Corps in action in 1945.

H1: IS-2m, 78th Guards Heavy Tank Regt.; Stuhl-weissenburg, Hungary, 1945

The regimental insignia, a Cyrillic 'D' in a diamond, is painted on the sides and rear of the turret, and there is a large, sloppily-painted tactical number. This was one of the IS-2 units involved in heavy fighting outside Budapest in the early months of 1945.

H2: IS-3M, Egyptian 4th Armoured Div.; Cairo, 1967

Tanks of this formation were often marked with large insignia for parades in Cairo, like the royal eagle or vulture painted in black on this Stalin. Such markings were seldom, if ever, carried into combat. The tank is finished in a light sand colour.

ISU-122S of the 2nd Byelorussian Front in the dock area of Gdansk, Poland, on 30 March 1945. Behind the tactical number '23' is the slogan 'In Honour of Mikoyan'. The hemispherical mantlet which distinguished the IS-122S from the -122 can just be seen. (Sovfoto)

Notes sur les planches en couleur

A1: Les rayures de couleur sur la tourelle indiquent le bataillon d'une brigade. (Encart) rayures utilisées uniquement sur la tourelle principale des T35 de la 34ème division blindée, 1941. **A2:** Réparé dans un atelier de Léningrad; 'Nous defendons les conquêtes d'Octobre' (la révolution d'Octobre 1917), a été peint sur ce tank.

B1: Monté à l'aide de pièces détachées au 27 ème Centre de Réparations de Léningrad, ce KV porte deux slogans: 'Pour Léningrad' et en dessous 'Pour le Front, de la part des femmes de Léningrad'. '716' ètait probablement les trois derniers chiffres du numéro de série de l'usine. **B2:** Le nom 'Shchortz' est en l'honneur d'un général bolchevique de 1917–20; l'indication tactique est '33', suivi de 'N'.

C1: Le slogan est 'La victoire nous appartient'. **C2:** *'Bezposhadni'*—'Sans merci'—un tank offert par la communauté artistique de Moscou et commandé par le lieutenant Khoroshilov. Les petites étoiles indiquent le nombre de canons et de tanks ennemis détruits. Il y a aussi huit lignes d'un poème de Kupriyanof, mais la traduction n'en fait pas un chef d'oeuvre!

D1: Le slogan '25 Octobre' évoque la date de la Révolution de 1917 d'après l'ancien calendrier Julien. **D2:** Tanks et avions ètaient fréquement appelés 'Nevskii' d'après le grand film patriotique d'Eisenstein, alors très populaire. '3' et '2' identifient probablement la brigade d'un corps blindé et le bataillon de la brigade. Le chiffre figurait aussi au centre de la caisse supérieur arrière.

E1: L'inscription 'les Fermiers de Chelyabinski' rappelle les contributions des paysans de la région des usines de tanks de Chelyabinski, dans l'Oural. **E2:** Le *hakaristi* ètait peint sur les deux côtés de la tourelle, le côté gauche de la tourelle arrière et sur l'écoutille—et au centre de la plaque supérieure arrière.

F1: Les rayures blanches furent peintes en avril 1945 pour faciliter l'identification par l'aviation alliée; le sanglier blanc et l'étoile rouge ètaient l'insigne du régiment; '434' indique le régiment, la 3ème compagnie et le 4ème tank. *'Boyevaya Podruga'* est peint sur la tourelle arrière—voir Vanguard No 14, *The T-34 Tank*, planche B2. **F2:** Voir détail des légendes numérotées accompagnant l'illustration.

G1: Couleur soviétique standard et emblème tchécoslovaque. **G2:** L'aigle blanc 'Piast', emblème national, ètait peint sur losange rouge; les rayures blanches sont pour la reconnaissance aérienne.

H1: Le 'D' sur losange est l'insigne du régiment, qui combattit aux abords de Budapest. **H2:** Emblèmes tels que cet aigle royal, ou vautour, ètaient rarement vus au combat.

Farbtafeln

A1: Bunte Streifen um den Turm lassen das Bataillon innerhalb der Brigade erkennen. (Eingesetzt) Die Streifen wurden nur am Hauptturm von T-35s der 34. Panzerdivision im Jahr 1941, benutzt. **A2:** In einer Leningrad Werkstatt repariert, dieser Panzer wurde mit dem Slogan bemalt 'Wir verteidigen die Eroberung vom Oktober'—gmeint war die Oktoberrevolution von 1917.

B1: Zusammengebaut aus Teilen im Leningrader 27. Panzer-Reparaturzentrum, dieser KV hat zwei Slogans—'Für Leningrad' darüber 'Der Front von den Leningrader Frauen'. '716' waren wahrscheinlich die letzten drei Stellen der Herstellerserienummer. **B2:** Der Name 'Shchortz' erinnert an einen bolschewistischen General von 1917–20; die taktische Markierung ist '33', gefolgt von einem 'N'.

C1: Der Slogan ist, 'Der Sieg wird uns gehören'. **C2:** *'Besposhadni'*—'Erbarmungslos' ein Panzer, bezahlt mit den Stiftungsgeldern von Moskaus Künstlergemeinde und kommandiert von Lt. Khoroshilov. Kleine Sterne representieren die zerstörten feindlichen Panzer und Geschütze. Ein acht-Zeilen Vers von Kupriyanof ist auch zur Schau gestellt: in der Übersetzung ist er peinlich schlecht!

D1: Der Slogan '25. Oktober' bezieht sich auf das Datum der Revolution im Jahr 1917, in Bezugnahme auf den alten julianischen Kalender. **D2:** 'Nevskii' war ein gewöhnlich benutzter Name für Panzer und Flugzeuge, der Popularität von Eisenstein's grossem patriotischem Film folgend, '3' und '2' lassen wahrscheinlich eine Brigade innerhalb eines Panzercorps erkennen und dementsprechend das Bataillon der Brigade. Die Nummer wiederholte sich in der Mitte auf dem oberen hinteren Rumpf.

E1: Die Inschrift 'Chelyabinski Bauern' markiert Stiftungen von Bauern aus der Nähe der Panzerfabriken von Chelyabinsk im Ural. **E2:** Das finnische *hakaristi* war auf beiden Turmseiten, der linken Seite auf der Turmrückseite und der Luke; und in die Mitte auf der oberen ruckwärtigen Rumpfplatte gemalt.

F1: Weisse Streifen war die Markierung zur Erkennung der Panzer durch Flugzeuge für den April 1945; der weisse Eber und der rote Stern waren die regimentalen Abzeichen; die '434' lassen das Regiment, die 3. Kompanie und den 4. Panzer erkennen. Hinten am Turm war *'Boyevaya Podruga'* aufgemalt—siehe Vanguard Nr. 14, *The T-34 Tank*, Tafel B2. **F2:** Siehe Aufschlüsselung im Begleittext zu den Tafeln.

G1: Einfaches sovietisches Farbschema mit tschechischem Hoheitszeichen. **G2:** Der weisse 'Piast' Adler, das Nationalzeichen, wurde auf roter Raute getragen die weissen Streifen sind zur Erkennung durch Flugzeuge.

H1: Das 'D' in einer Raute ist das Regimentsabzeichen. Diese Einheit Kämpfte ausserhalb von Budapest. **H2:** Abzeichen wie dieser königliche Adler, oder Geier wurden selten im Kampf gesehen.